After reading this book, you'll be able to turn your work group into an effective team by helping it manage what it does and how it does it; by helping it develop open, honest, and direct communication; and by helping it resolve conflicts and solve problems.

Other Titles in the Successful Office Skills Series

Becoming an Effective Leader
Building Better Relationships on the Job
Coaching and Counseling in the Workplace
Conflict Resolution
Creative Problem Solving
Get Organized! How to Control Your Life Through Self-Management
How to Be a Successful Interviewer
How to Be a Successful Manager
How to Deal With Difficult People
How to Delegate Effectively
How to Get the Best Out of People
How to Make an Effective Speech or Presentation
How to Negotiate a Raise or Promotion
How to Read Financial Statements
How to Run a Meeting
How to Write Easily and Effectively
How to Write an Effective Résumé
Improve Your Reading Power
Increasing Your Memory Power
Making Tough Decisions
Managing Stress
Polishing Your Professional Image
Winning on the Telephone

Effective Team Building

Donald H. Weiss

amacom
American Management Association
New York • Atlanta • Boston • Chicago • Kansas City • San Francisco • Washington, D.C.
Brussels • Toronto • Mexico City

This book is available at a special discount when ordered in bulk quantities. For information, contact Special Sales Department, AMACOM, a division of American Management Association, 135 West 50th Street, New York, NY 10020.

Library of Congress Cataloging-in-Publication Data

Weiss, Donald H., 1936–
Effective team building / Donald H. Weiss.
p. cm.—(The Successful office skills series)
Includes bibliographical references (p.) and index.
ISBN 0-8144-7819-0
1. Work groups. I. Title. II. Series.
HD60.W448 1993
658.4'02—dc20 *93-16043*
CIP

Printing number

10 9 8 7 6 5 4 3 2 1

CONTENTS

INTRODUCTION

You can't call every work group a team, and you can't assume that a team is effective simply because it is a team. How about where you work? Is your work unit a team? Is it really effective?

Did you answer no to either question? If you did, this book probably can help you and the other people in your work group get with a program for creating an effective team.

Creating an effective team doesn't mean that everyone in your work unit has to work on different parts of one project. However, everyone does have to work toward the same goals and objectives. Focusing all the team's energies on those goals and objectives, regardless of members' specific jobs, produces what we call "synergy": the coming together of everyone's efforts to achieve whatever results you shoot for. And synergy is what makes a team effective.

This book will help you create synergy. In it we'll show you some of the steps you need to take—from forming a team to resolving conflicts and solving problems.

CHAPTER ONE

Is Your Work Unit a Team?

Andy Sanchez, an assembly group supervisor, stood in the back of the lunchroom listening intently to the speeches from the top brass and feeling pleased and excited that Warren Manufacturing, the company for which he had worked for the last eight years, had landed two new contracts to build steel forms and structural components for high-rise office buildings being built downtown. The competition had been fierce, but his company, with its record for meeting or beating deadlines, had won.

"With these two new contracts, Warren Manufacturing is entering a new phase of growth," Marjorie Williams declared from the cleared space in the packed lunchroom. "And, as I look around this room, I see the team that will lead us into the year two thousand. You—'Team Warren'—all of you have made us what we are."

"Team Warren"? The phrase gave Andy a moment's shocked pause. What team? He looked around the room at the people that the company's controller had just called "Team Warren" and wondered what she was seeing that he wasn't.

"Three hundred and eighty-five people, that's what I see," Andy mused. "Most of them are so new, I don't even know half of them. White people, black people, Latinos, Asians—they all have their own thing. And of those I know, I'd stand up for only eight of them—my assembly group.

" 'Team Warren'? Look over there. There's Manny standing against the wall. Go to his parts room for angle irons or bits, and see how much of a team there is. You'd think he owned the joint, that the parts were his. How about Shirley, in personnel? Every time you go to her with a medical claim, it's like you're asking her to pony up the money from her own pocket. And I'll stand up for my people, but will they stand up for me?

"It seems like everyone's out for himself or protecting his or her own turf. People will pull together only as long as Warren's putting food on their tables. If we hadn't gotten those contracts, it would've been 'So long, sweetheart' from most of them. That woman sure has a different slant on things than I do."

Have you ever had these same doubts about your company? Is it really a team? Can it ever become a team? How about your own work group? Is it a team? If it is, what makes it so? If it isn't, what can you do to foster teamwork?

Andy has put his finger on a number of difficult issues surrounding the notion of teams and of team building—one of the new darlings of management theory and practices. The people at Warren, many of them relatively new hires, don't know one another and don't share much of a common history. They seem self-absorbed, more caught up with private or ethnic-group concerns than with common interests and values. They've been brought together to meet a specific set of relatively short-term goals and objectives—to fulfill the two new contracts—but beyond that, they have little loyalty to their organization. Andy's probably right when he asks, "What team?"

Teamwork benefits everyone in the work group—each person, as well as the supervisor and the group as a whole. But not every group that calls itself a team benefits everyone to the same extent; some teams are more effective than others. The keys to effective teamwork include recognizing and managing the team's dynamics, communicating effectively and encouraging collaboration, and managing (rather than suppressing) conflicts and other problems that arise.

Characteristics of a Team

Unless you work in a very small company, it's difficult to call your whole company a team. Everyone in the company has a common long-term goal: making the company profitable. But that's as far as it goes. The entire work force of a large company is too large to coalesce around short-term goals or objectives and common interests, values, or history.

The accompanying box lists the criteria that separate a team from a mere crowd of people.

A team is smaller than a company. Let's use a sports analogy. A baseball team—twenty-five active players—constitutes a part of the company known as the ______ (you fill in the blank with your favorite team name). Some people refer to the team as the company's product: "The Chicago

---

What Makes a Team a Team?

A team is a relatively small group of people formed around common interests, values, and history and brought together to meet a specific set of relatively short-term goals or objectives.

Cubs field one of the best teams in baseball—on paper." The Cubs' *organization* is vast—with front-office people, back-office people, top-office people, radio people, TV people, farm people, and on and on and on. Each group within the organization may also be a team—e.g., the front-office team. The most we can say about a company is that it is an organization of teams.

Not every group of people is a team, even if they work together under a common name, such as the assembly unit. To become a team, a relatively small group of people must form around common interests, values, and history. Team members come to know each other very well and recognize each other's strengths and weaknesses, abilities and needs. At the least, they must have a shared interest in putting out the product or service for which their group is responsible. They must value the same quantity or quality of output, the same outcomes in terms of return on their effort, and the same recognition for the work that they do. They develop a common history based on doing similar things within the group, learning how to do those things over time, and passing through essentially the same process to get to a given position within the group.

To continue our baseball illustration, very few players jump directly from high school to the big leagues. They usually undergo rigorous training in the farm system, passing upward through levels of proficiencies and moving through grades in the system as they learn, not only the skills of baseball, but also the "culture" of the business.

Your work unit and the job you do meet needs created by the organization, and the unit's and your objectives serve the mission of the organization; the organization can change all of these at will. So, too, with a team. You can change your team's objectives without affecting the character of the whole organization, but you can't change the organization's goals without affecting the character of the teams within it. That's why we say that a team's objectives are relatively short-term.

A baseball team on the field is brought together to meet a specific set of relatively short-term goals or objectives—win the World Series by winning more games than any other team. If, by the end of September, it looks as if the team won't even win its division title, then the organization can change the team's objective, revising it to call for ending the season in second place. In some instances, the team's place in the standings may be irrelevant, and building for the future may become the team's objective. The organization's goals, however, remain the same: make a profit and build fan loyalty.

Andy's group, his assembly team, also has very specific short-term goals or objectives. Read what he says to Fred Robinson, a new but experienced employee, headed to the team to help meet the demands created by the recently won contracts.

Andy: Our job's pretty simple, but it's also important. We have to assemble these joints just right, or the whole structure will collapse. One weak rivet, one bolt not tightened down just right—it'll shear, and the whole thing will come down. You know what that means?

Fred: A lotta people can get hurt.

Andy: Killed. And not just our guys, either, and not necessarily right away. A bad joint might last five minutes or five years. You can't ever know.

Fred: That's a big responsibility.

Andy: Very big. Now, we have to produce ten thousand of these joints in the next six months. You should be able to turn out one of these joints in about fifteen minutes—ninety to one hundred a day, once you get into a rhythm. Here's your work order board for today. If you have any questions and I'm not around, ask Mac there. He started right at this station himself, so he knows exactly what to do and how to do it right. If you have any questions ask them.

Fred: No, I haven't any questions.

This dialogue reflects every characteristic of a team. (You can use these same criteria to decide whether your work unit is, in fact, a team.) Andy's team is:

- A relatively small group (now nine people plus Andy)
- Formed around common interests (steel working), values (safe joints), and history (trained in the job and on the same equipment)
- Brought together to meet a specific set of relatively short-term goals or objectives (in this project, to produce 10,000 joints in six months)

So the question isn't whether Andy's group is a team. Rather, the question is whether Andy's team is an effective team. If your work unit is a team, you can now ask the same question.

CHAPTER TWO

What Makes a Team Effective?

We say that an efficient person is one who does a job the right way. An effective person is one who does the *right* job the right way, that is, meets a predetermined objective using appropriate methods. Effective teams are like effective people.

Effective teams operate in an environment in which well-trained people can accomplish their goals or objectives without a designated head, that is, without a supervisor. Few teams reach that level of effectiveness, although many companies today are looking to create them. Short of self-management, work units like Andy's and, probably, yours can improve the level of teamwork if everyone, from supervisor on down, takes a fresh look at how everyone works together to accomplish the unit's objectives. Read the following dialogue to get a sense of what we're talking about.

Andy: Thanks for staying a little late, guys. We have a problem. The number 2 joint is not fitting right, and we need to put our heads together over it. We might not solve it tonight, but we can begin thinking about it. Maybe we'll come back in the morning with some new ideas.

Mac: We all went over the specs. Are the parts milled wrong?

Andy: Could be.

Fred: I was working on them today. Could I have put them together wrong?

Andy: I don't know.

Sue: I was working on them, too. I can put them together in my sleep.

Stan: Are those the joints over there in that bin?

Andy: Yes. They're all off.

Stan: Why don't we all take one home tonight and take a look at it? Let's see what we come up with.

Al: I've got a scout meeting with my boys tonight, but I guess I can look at a joint when I get back.

Mac: This should be simple to solve. I'll take one, too.

This dialogue indicates several key characteristics of effective teams: a sense of commitment (everyone agreed to stay a few minutes late), a high degree of communication within the group (everyone who had an idea spoke up freely), agreement through consensus (everyone agreed to take a unit home and to take personal time to come up with a solution to an apparent problem), and a sense of empowerment (everyone believed that the unit members, personally and as a group, could solve the problem). These characteristics are most but not all of what makes a team effective. You'll find a complete list in the accompanying box.

Characteristics of an Effective Team

- A sense of commitment
- A high degree of communication within the group and with people outside the group
- A healthy degree of disagreement and creativity
- Agreement through consensus
- A sense of empowerment

Commitment

How responsible do you feel for what your work group does? Team members must feel responsible for what the team does, as well as for what they individually contribute if the team is to be effective. If you're a supervisor, you can order people to work or offer them rewards or threaten them with punishments, but unless they want to make a contribution or want to care for what the group achieves, they are at best complying with your wishes, that is, merely obeying orders. The danger with demanding compliance and obedience is that, if workers begin to feel resentful, their compliance can turn into *malicious obedience:* "I'll do it, but I'll sabotage you or the group in the process." People become committed to a group, a process, or an idea only if they see that commitment as being in their best interest.

The old notion of WIIFM (what's-in-it-for-me, pronounced whiff-'em) plays a large part in commitment. When people anticipate a payoff, whether tangible (e.g., a bonus) or intangible (e.g., recognition), for making a commitment, they are more likely to give the team's activities the effort they deserve. If they see little or no value for them in the team's activities, they soon give up their work on the team or turn on their leaders. What's it worth to you to become committed to the team's future?

Communication

Effective teams communicate—openly, directly, and honestly—within the group and with others outside the group. If people within the team don't talk to each other, teamwork and productivity suffer. Remember, in Chapter 1, how Andy invited Fred to ask questions about his job and the team's functioning. That's communication, a key ingredient in any effective team.

As you look around your work group, ask yourself how much people talk with each other and with the group's supervisor. I don't mean just small talk, although that's important. I mean shop talk related to problem solving and decision making. That kind of big talk makes a group a team.

Disagreement and Creativity

Open, honest, and direct communication is going to breed disagreement, and team leaders and team members alike want not only to tolerate it, but also to encourage it. Only when people look at a given situation from different perspectives and then discuss those perspectives can minor problems be solved before they become crises. That's what we mean by being proactive rather than reactive, being creative rather than gridlocked.

The brief meeting of Andy's team the next morning illustrates what we're talking about.

Mac: I think the rivets are off on the cross member. They came that way from the vendor.

Sue: That's not what I came up with. Look at the holes here on this piece. They're off by a hair, just enough to throw the whole assembly out of line.

Stan: Well, I don't know. Neither one of those things should make a difference.

Fred: What if they're both off at the same time?

Andy: Let's take a look. Hmm. You may be right, Fred. Why don't you three—Mac, Sue, and Fred—take a unit apart? Then reassemble it and see what you come up with. Al, Stan—we need to talk with the vendors if we're right.

No one was afraid to disagree with other team members. All spoke their opinions in a frank and direct manner, and no one took offense at the disagreement. The upshot was a fresh look at the problem—and a probable solution. Could a conversation like that occur in your workplace? If not, why not?

Agreement Through Consensus

You have probably noticed that, although the whole process for handling the team's problem has been quite democratic, no one has been asked for a vote. Majority rule has become synonymous with democracy, but, throughout human history, majority rule has also been associated with majority tyranny. Minority opinions, no matter how correct, have been suppressed by the majority; minority rights, no matter how well guarded, have been abridged by the majority. True democracy calls, not for majority rule, but for consensus—the process by which the members of the team all express their own opinions before agreeing to try a procedure or to live with an idea until it proves unworkable or untenable.

Whereas voting characterizes majority rule, debate characterizes consensus. Quick decisions can come from majority rule, but more effective decisions come from taking the time to reach consensus. To achieve consensus, all group members are required to support their ideas with data or to make measurable or observable predictions. Even if you say, "The only reason I think we should do this is a gut feeling," the idea is worthy of consideration as long as the outcome can be tested. If everyone agrees to go along with your idea, then time and reality will test its value.

How does your group solve problems and make decisions? If you're not operating by consensus now, ask the group to try this form of decision making instead of taking a vote. It could dramatically change the quality of your work life.

Empowerment

To get people to accept responsibility for group actions, as well as for their own actions, people must feel that they have the power to influence decisions and actions that affect their lives. No one in Andy's group feels left out or powerless, which contributes to making his team work together well—at least up to this point.

Power means the ability to control what happens. From feeding yourself as a child to feeding your family as an adult, you feel good about yourself only if you can satisfy your needs through your own effort. Powerlessness destroys teamwork. If people feel that the group has taken away their own ability to think for themselves, to take action, to influence the group's activities and outcomes, and to initiate change, teamwork will be destroyed. Full participation is the only antidote to powerlessness.

If people feel they have power to control their own lives, they will do whatever has to be done. Ask the employees of Kellogg Foods, Corning Glass, Johnsonville Foods, 3M, or Hewlett Packard. These industrial leaders have all created environments conducive to full participation.

So what makes a team an effective team? Doing the *right* job the right way—that is, meeting objectives through appropriate methods and in an environment in which well-trained people can accomplish their goals or objectives—if necessary, without a supervisor.

CHAPTER THREE

How Teamwork Benefits You and Your Organization

"Teamwork" has become a buzzword in management jargon. There's little doubt that teamwork improves the quality of work life, increases productivity, reduces costs, and improves the quality of the organization's products or services. But not every situation calls for teamwork.

When to Create a Team

You should build a team only when a team is likely to outperform an individual or a group of individuals working separately. For example, if a high degree of technical skill is needed and only one person has that skill, a demand for teamwork clearly makes no sense. If speed is crucial you don't have time to debate the pros and cons of how the job should be done; teams would only get in the way as long as you have one or two people necessary for getting the job done *right* and getting the job done *now.*

Research and practice both demonstrate that, when appropriate, teamwork raises the quality of the decisions made and the actions taken, while lowering the risk of failure. It increases the group's level of commitment to the decisions and the actions, and it enhances the lives of the individual group members, their supervisors, and their organizations. We saw this in action in Chapter 2, when Andy's group members put their heads together to solve a problem. Two people had different ideas concerning what was wrong. Two other people helped them pull their ideas together. As a group, they succeeded where, as individuals, they might have gone off into dead ends.

Benefits of Teamwork

When teamwork is appropriate, everyone benefits—you as a team member, you as a supervisor, and the whole organization.

Benefits to the Individual: When you work in a team, you'll find your work to be less stressful because both the work and the responsibility for success are shared. Members of effective teams recognize and support one another. They all share in any recognition that the team receives from external sources. And they all feel a sense of belonging, which is an important internal reward. They feel a sense of accomplishment and a sense of self-fulfillment that individuals working alone cannot.

Benefits to the Supervisor: Look at what Andy got out of bringing the flawed joint to the group. Not only did the group solve the problem, it wound up with increased productivity, improved cost/benefit ratios (profitability), improved morale, and improved loyalty and retention. What more can you, as a supervisor, ask for? How about less stress and more recognition from upper management? All that should make you feel pretty good about building an effective team.

Benefits to the Organization: Industrial leaders tend to encourage teamwork among their employees. Companies like Hewlett Packard have replaced centrally controlled divisions with independent businesses in which groups of engineers, marketers, trainers, support personnel, and even vendors are brought together and trained to function as teams. Together, they produce the best possible products and bring them to market at the lowest cost possible. Increased productivity and creativity translate directly to the bottom line. Stop here for a moment, and make a list of ways in which your company could benefit from more teamwork in the ranks.

Barriers to Teamwork

"A camel is a horse put together by a committee." Have you ever heard that around your shop? The ongoing popularity of that old chestnut reflects the anxiety of some individuals, supervisors, and organizations about creating work teams to replace individual producers. Unions fear that their members will be co-opted by managers; managers fear that their jobs will become superfluous; and organizations fear that individual producers will begin thinking for themselves and create dissension.

Barriers Created by the Individual: Individual nonmanagement employees often feel threatened and are afraid of losing status and becoming lost in the crowd if they become part of a team. They fear missing out on recognition, rewards, and promotions if they are seen merely as members of a team. They also sometimes fear taking responsibility for their own actions, of having to answer to other people for what they do. They therefore resist teamwork.

Barriers Created by the Supervisor: "If I create this team, what will I do? How will I control my personnel and productivity?" These are questions frequently asked by supervisors who fear losing power or status. Such supervisors often do not delegate responsibility and authority properly. Sometimes they punish the team for taking the initiative. Some managers have been known to sabotage the team by failing to make resources available when needed: "See, I told you it would never work."

Barriers Created by the Organization: "Managers think; producers do." This second old chestnut also stands in the way of effective teams. Managers have created layers of "thinkers" within the organization that often get in the way of creativity, innovation, and the ability to take rapid action in the face of major industrial, technological, or social changes. Bureaucracy creates barriers to teamwork by using top-down management.

Other barriers can be found in any kind of organization. Rewards and compensation may be distributed unfairly, as when top managers receive more than one hundred times the compensation of first-line employees. Managers may fail to set clear and well-defined goals and objectives, or they may fail to communicate those goals and objectives to all employees. Supervisors may fail to build effective teams because they don't see themselves as leaders as well as managers.

Team Leadership

Supervisors are appointed by management to head groups. The true leaders, however, are elected by the group, either openly or tacitly. You don't have to be a supervisor to be a leader. That different people can take leadership roles at different times helps make teams effective.

Group Managers: Supervisors are appointed by managers to take charge of (be responsible for) the productivity of a group. They are usually nominated on the basis of their expertise and often have admirable administrative skills. But, because they are usually selected on the basis of their technical skills, they often have very few leadership skills.

Leaders: Leaders have the ability to influence or persuade other people, to provide them with direction, and to urge them to think and to do what they otherwise would not think or do on their own. For whatever reason—their expertise, their warmth and charm, their charisma—leaders get people to back them when it counts. Leaders provide a model for behavior and exemplify all the values of the group. They impart vision to the group, whether it be as simple as, "We're going to be the best assembly group in the company" or as ambitious as, "We're going to capture the largest market share in the industry." They encourage communication and collaboration. They help people feel good about the group and what the group is doing, and they help integrate all the characteristics of effective groups into their team's process.

Anyone can be a leader. In self-managed teams (teams that organize and supervise their own internal workings), people assume leadership roles appropriate to their functions or expertise. What a person does and how he or she relates to other people determine leadership.

So, blessed are the supervisors who are also leaders. They combine the virtues of great administrative skills with the qualities of leadership to build effective teams.

Everyone benefits from an environment that encourages teamwork—not just in clearly defined work groups, but also in cross-departmental groups that work together to bring a complex product or service to market. Everyone who participates will take away at least as much as he or she gives to the group, and usually more.

CHAPTER FOUR

How to Form a Team

Andy Sanchez didn't handpick his work group (except for Fred, whom he just hired). Andy received a promotion and inherited a work group. That's usually how a team gets started. Sometimes, however, you get lucky and are asked to form a team around a short-term objective where before no team existed at all. Then you can handpick your team members and set the ground rules from scratch. In either case, the group *evolves* into a team, but only through the conscious efforts of its members.

Team Formation and Development

Whether developing within an existing work group or forming from scratch, all teams experience the phases described in the accompanying box. At various times and in various ways, all teams pass through six predictable steps. Different teams experience these phases in different ways, in different sequences, and in a variety of tempos (which is why we are reluctant to call this process a cycle). Your team (especially if it's an ad hoc voluntary group, such as a short-lived project team) can get to Step 5, Producing, quickly, sometimes in a matter of hours. If yours is a new work unit or if you've just become a new supervisor, getting the preliminaries out of the way can take days; in longer-lived groups, these stages can

Phases of Team Development

Introducing:	Coming together as a group
Stage setting:	Laying the ground rules; creating the climate
Probing/ testing:	Getting to know one another; establishing positions within the group; developing trust, candor
Creating	Identifying objectives; solving problems; designing methods for doing business
Producing	Executing the team's functions
Maintaining	Taking care of continuation needs

reoccur every time a new person or a new objective is introduced into the team. You and everyone else on the team should facilitate the process by openly identifying what is happening as it occurs; doing so helps prevent problems that could get out of hand.

Just as the tempo can vary from group to group, so, too, can the climate. Some groups enjoy trust and candor, with little or no interpersonal conflict; opinions are expressed openly and honestly, no one gets upset or disturbed, and the positive and productive feelings the people share are genuine and sincere. Other groups struggle continuously, rancor or conflict shred the team's fabric, and, even if the team accomplishes its objectives, the bad feelings linger. How a group comes to grip with these facts of team life often depends upon how well the group leader sets the stage. Let's look at each phase in more detail.

Introducing: Team members meet and gather information about each other's backgrounds, values, skills, and interests. Polite, superficial (usually work-related) conversations deal mainly with recent backgrounds and other items that satisfy members' curiosity about who people are and what roles they might play within the group: what-do-you-bring-to-the-party type of questions.

Stage Setting: If you're the supervisor or project manager, you explain the group's objectives or mandate and other business requirements and establish the ground rules for how the team will function. One way to do that is by modeling behavior (acting in the manner in which you expect team members to act), rather than telling people what to do. By word or by deed, the leader structures the group's behavior.

If you're the leader, you create the team's tone or climate; what you do or say directs the team's behavior. If you tell people you want them to be full participants in team development, they will nod, smile politely, and seriously doubt every word you say. Involving them in organizing and directing the team's activities demonstrates that you really mean them to be involved.

In an ad hoc voluntary team, you can be as flexible and as open to suggestion as you want, because the team's mandate prescribes few roles. In work units or appointed teams, the roles are usually more structured; focusing on how to fulfill the team's mandate rather than on what that mandate is allows team members to participate in the decisions that could affect their lives. How you conduct yourself usually teaches people what you expect them to do and how you expect them to act toward you, toward each other, and toward the team's mission.

Probing/testing: Probing and testing go on all the time, whether you realize it or not. To get to know other people, you need to probe beyond the superficialities of introductions to understand people's values, needs, and interests—to find out where they "are coming from," what they expect to get out of the team and out of one another, and how they personally will benefit from the team's success. By doing this, you're testing each other's strengths and weaknesses or each other's dedication to the team's goals and objectives. Comfort and trust levels vary with how you perceive each other and how you "mesh" with one another.

Probing gets beneath the surface, the veneer of sociability, and can make you feel uncomfortable. However, resisting efforts to get close and engaging in self-protective, guarded behavior can block team growth. Candor and openness do not come easily; you have to encourage and nurture them.

Part of this probing comes from the human need for affiliation. You've probably experienced the need to feel linked more intimately to others than merely "belonging to the group." You therefore set about to make linkages with other individuals, sometimes creating a "we-them" situation within the group. You look for allies, for other people with whom you can identify or to whom you can relate—people who think and feel the way you do. You take sides with other people, make "friends" with some, separate yourself from others. It's easier to trust and be candid with one person than to open yourself up to a whole group.

You also test each other's need to dominate or to influence the group. You identify whom you can influence. You test the strengths of the group's influencers, people who seem to know what they are saying or doing (whether or not they do). People often acquiesce easily to others who seem to know what they are talking about, who seem to have experience that the team can use, or who merely wear down the group with the force of their personality or opinions.

Since all of this interpersonal sizing up and testing goes on and can occur at any time in the life of a team, it's best that you be aware that they're happening. Anything that blocks team growth, if ignored or left to work itself out, can tear apart a group.

Creating: Forming a new team or presenting a team with new objectives calls for creative thinking and even innovation. How you and the other team members manage the team's dynamics will affect how people identify their tasks and the obstacles they face on their way to success. If you're the leader and dictate to the group or make outrageous demands at this point, you will produce compliance, rather than commitment to problem solving or to achieving the group's goals. If you permit or encourage innovation, the team will work at being innovative; if you permit or encourage the team to solve its own production problems, the team will work at being more productive. On the other hand, if you call all the shots, answer all the questions, and solve all the problems—or just give the appearance of holding a tight rein—you will drain the team's creative energies and create an atmosphere of anger, resentment, and apathy.

Producing: Your team may be highly creative and energetic, but it can never forget that its objectives are the reasons for which the team has been created. After all the testing, planning, and creativity comes the time to produce or disband. Effective teams establish norms—explicit or implicit rules or understandings that prescribe who will do what, when, and where—that make its work possible. Those norms become the basis for the group's functioning until another demand for change appears.

Maintaining: Your team will perform well only if everyone takes steps to support the behaviors and dynamics that make a team successful: task maintenance (e.g., administrative details, production needs, delivery needs) and process maintenance (e.g., group dynamics, communication needs).

Someone has to watch what is happening within the team and take action to adjust or fine-tune the group's functioning. The team leader can monitor the team or ask the team to monitor itself; whichever happens in your team, the team leader is ultimately responsible for the team's maintenance. The leader's confidence in the team's abilities shows in how that person leads the team.

Especially if you are the group manager, if you get behind the team and try to drive it toward accomplishing its business goals, it will take on a task orientation, satisfying your demands, rather than generating its own solutions. On the other hand, if you allow the group to drag out the process of becoming a team, it will take on a process orientation that might prevent its satisfying the business demands for which it was created. The two drivers of all business group dynamics—task and process—determine the direction the group will take. (See Chapter 5.)

Forming a Team From Scratch

Whether or not you're a management employee, it's not unlikely that you'll be asked at one time or another to form a team. In Chapter 2, Andy asked Mac, Sue, and Fred to form an ad hoc, very short-lived team to test their ideas about the malfunctioning joint.

When forming a more enduring team from scratch, you need to select people carefully; the mix can determine the effectiveness of the team. You have to take into account skills, previous experience with and commitment to teamwork, interpersonal skills, and degree of self-selection.

Skills: A business team has a task-oriented goal to achieve; that's its reason for being. Skills are needed for achieving that goal. When selecting people for the team, you have to ensure that the skills are there—or if they're not there, that the people you select are capable of learning them in short order.

Previous Experience With and Commitment to Teamwork: Gifted loners are legendary, and in many instances they are not sufficiently appreciated, but they can wreak havoc with a team. Selecting people for their ability to cooperate with one another is important to the success of the team, but that can't always be done. Forming a product development team may require you to bring together a top-flight engineer, a crackerjack marketing pro, a project manager with a fanatical eye for detail, and so on. Some of these people are probably accustomed to working on their own. When selecting your team members, you will have to begin guiding them into new relationships, some of which will be uncomfortable for them. However, a commitment to work together is at stake. The "how-to" will follow.

Interpersonal Skills: Your most effective team members will come to the table with excellent interpersonal skills, especially with a willingness to cooperate. You will want to emphasize these skills in your selection criteria. But, again, that's not always possible. We come back, therefore, to the need for a commitment to work together.

Self-selection: Self-selection is a two-edged sword. Although you want people to volunteer for the team, those who do often do not have the kind of skills you're looking for. On the other hand, volunteers usually feel a high degree of interest in the team's objectives and commitment to its success. Self-selection during role assignments, however, facilitates the process of getting the work done, which we discuss in Chapter 5.

Teamwork Development

We have said that evolving a team from an ordinary work group or from scratch takes a conscious effort on everyone's part. Even if you're the team manager, you may not be able to manage all things the group needs to do (e.g., correcting communication problems, building coalitions, group problem solving, and decision making), but here are a few things anyone can do to initiate teamwork.

- *Hold informational meetings.* If you're the team leader, you should initiate the introductory process, using listening exercises. However, anyone can sit and talk with anyone else to get to know each other over lunch or during a break. If you're the leader of a newly formed team, you can hold a meeting early in the life of the group in which team members pair up and interview each other about their lives, their skills, and their expectations for and of the group. Then each person can introduce the partner he or she interviewed to the whole group.

▪ *Contribute to productive meetings.* Every group should hold meetings concerning its goals and objectives (including discussions of expectations and reservations). If the meetings are to be productive, team members should compare actual progress to those goals and objectives. Suggestions for sustaining positive results or for taking corrective action can then be generated and implemented.

▪ *Self-select roles.* We mentioned that self-selection of roles facilitates group dynamics and spurs progress toward goals. During productive meetings, you will want to volunteer, or encourage others, to take on important tasks that need to be done. The more you and others help the group by sharing responsibilities, the more successful the group will be.

▪ *Share ideas.* Andy's group works together well because members willingly share their ideas. Mac didn't come to his boss for a private discussion of a possible solution to the problem with the joint. Neither did Sue nor Stan. They brainstormed in a very short but successful discussion.

▪ *Facilitate meetings.* An excellent way to develop teamwork is for everyone in the group to take a crack at facilitating group meetings. Instead of having the team manager always sit at the head of the table during a meeting, different team members take the chair and moderate the process. He or she is responsible for the agenda, for achieving the meeting's objectives, and for communicating the meeting's results to everyone.

Teams don't just happen. They take care and nurturing. Taking the team through its formation processes is one way to create a team; developing the group's ability to function as a team is another.

CHAPTER FIVE

How to Make Your Team More Effective

Andy's group solved the problem of the misfit joint: The predrilled holes were out of line, and the vendor replaced the parts. The time lost, however, set them back with respect to their production schedule.

Andy: We're a whole week behind now. We need to catch up. Any ideas?

Al: If you're talking about overtime, forget it.

Andy: I just asked for ideas.

Al: I'm not working overtime.

Mac: What do we need to do, Andy?

Andy: We need to get back on track. As I said, we're a week behind.

Al: No overtime for me.

Mac: Any other suggestion, Al?

Al: No.

Mac: Anyone else have any problems with overtime? [*No one answers.*] That leaves just you out of the overtime, Al.

Sue: I've been doing some arithmetic, and think if we each added 15 percent to our regular quotas, we might get by without overtime. How do you feel about that?

Fred: Since I'm new, I don't know if I can keep up with you.

Phil: With your experience? I've seen you work. You can do it. We can all do it.

Mac: If we do that, then each person will be responsible if he or she has to work overtime. How does that fly with you, Andy?

Andy: I'd need to know early enough in the day to get the overtime approved. You know the rules; I have to stay if any hourly employee stays late, and I have to let my family know. Any other ideas?

Fred: What time is 'early enough'? I might be the one staying late.

Andy: Let's say by 2:30. How's that, Al?

Al: I don't know. Fifteen percent's a lot. So we're behind. So what?

Sue: We have targets to hit.

Al: So? It won't kill the company if we miss a couple of targets.

Mac: No. But we have the best production record in the company, and I, for one, don't want to see that record spoiled.

Stan: Me, neither.

Al: Ah, so what?

Mac: It's a matter of pride, Al.

Sue: And productivity bonus.

Al: Okay. Okay. Fifteen percent. But I'm not working overtime.

Andy: Any other ideas? [*No one answers.*] Then, it's agreed. Each of you will add 15 percent to your production levels every day this week. If you need to work overtime, you'll let me know by 2:30 on the day you need it. I'll get it approved, and I'll stay with you. Remember that you can't take more than six hours overtime in the week. Anyone disagree or have a problem with this arrangement?

Mac: No sweat, Andy. We'll catch up.

Andy: You guys did a great job. Thanks for your help. I personally appreciate it.

Al created several roadblocks to team effectiveness. First is "lone-wolfing"—he ignored group standards or goals. Second is "blocking out"—he was not listening to, or tuning out, other people. Third is "bullying" and "carping"—he was inconsiderate of other people's needs and needling and looking for problems in the ideas other people offer. In short, he was considering his own personal needs to the exclusion of the team's.

The others managed the team's activities very effectively, with Andy giving them room to take control. They offered opinions, they provided information, they suggested solutions, they supported one another, and they maintained the group's standards. Andy tested for consensus, and that's how they made their decision.

This dialogue demonstrates what it takes to make a team effective: everyone takes a hand in managing *what* it does and *how* it does it. We call those the team's *task* and *process* dynamics.

Task Dynamics

A team achieves its goals only by doing what has to be done. Not only must the team leader be aware of what the team is doing, everyone else on the team must be, also. Here are eighteen things you and your teammates can do to manage the team's task effectiveness:

1. *Managing activities.* Chair a meeting, coordinate or manage resources, and you're managing the team's activities. Andy chaired the meeting, and Sue coordinated the team's resources by doing the arithmetic they needed for making a decision.

2. *Initiating.* Andy called the meeting, and, in his own blunt way, Al made the suggestion—not to work overtime—that forced the group to look for an acceptable alternative. These are initiating activities, as are making suggestions, proposing new ideas, and getting activities started.

3. *Seeking information.* Mac's question, "What do you think we need to do, Andy?" was seeking information. You seek information when you ask questions for clarification or for ascertaining the accuracy of data.

4. *Giving information.* Sue gave information when she offered the percentage increase she figured out. Any time you offer data such as those, you're giving information.

5. *Seeking opinions.* Andy managed this aspect of teamwork by calling the meeting in the first place. He could have just told his group, "Everyone'll work overtime this week." Just how far do you think he would have gotten, especially with Al? When you ask other people for their views or their values or ask them to decide on the

relative merits of an idea or a generalization, you are seeking their opinions.

6. *Expressing opinions.* When you state your views or express your values or decide on the relative merits of an idea or a generalization, you're expressing your opinion. Al felt no reluctance to voice his feelings, which shows that Andy's team is working well. In another environment, Al might have felt too intimidated to speak out.

7. *Brainstorming.* Brainstorming is one way for a group to get all its information and opinions into the open, generating new or different ideas. By allowing everyone to express ideas without fear of being shot down, the process facilitates creativity and innovation.

8. *Elaborating.* When you interpret, explain, or explicate facts or opinions or draw conclusions from the data available, you're elaborating. Stan did that when he told Fred that he didn't think that he'd have any trouble reaching the new goals.

9. *Shaping or orienting.* From the start, Andy oriented the group: The team was behind in meeting its production goals. You can shape or orient the group by identifying progress toward goals, by defining positions, or by organizing activity.

10. *Summarizing.* You can summarize at any time during a meeting or a discussion in several different ways. Andy did it at the end by pulling together the group's suggestions. You can also summarize by pulling together related ideas or opinions and restating them or by coordinating activities of subgroups or group members.

11. *Seeking consensus.* It's a good idea to summarize when managing the process of seeking

consensus, polling the group for its readiness to make decisions or resolve disagreements. Mac did this when he asked, "Anyone else got any problems with overtime?"

12. *Taking consensus.* Andy took consensus when he asked for more ideas and no one ventured any. You take consensus when you ask that a decision be made or that issues be resolved. The group formulates a position and agrees to abide by its decisions. Consensus taking is not voting. When a group operates by consensus, everyone has to be willing to at least try out a decision until it proves unworkable.

13. *Setting standards.* You set standards by establishing criteria for evaluating ideas, opinions, decisions, products, or services. Andy's group already had a production standard, which, it is quite clear, was very important to the group members. The group then set a temporary standard by adding 15 percent to its quotas—and let Al know that his ideas or opinions concerning meeting those standards wouldn't wash with the group.

14. *Evaluating.* The group evaluated Al's opinions on the basis of what was best for the team: pride and productivity bonuses. You evaluate ideas by measuring them against the group's standards, just as Andy's team did.

15. *Producing.* You have to manage the team's tasks and do its work, or else your team will fail in its mission for the organization, whether you produce something or offer services. Andy's team wants to achieve its stated targets and will take whatever steps necessary to do so.

16. *Reporting.* Andy will write up the results

of this meeting and enter them into his own records. He will also send his report to his supervisor. You or someone else should take notes of meetings, write production reports, and complete any other required paperwork.

17. *Representing.* Andy will send on his report, first, to let his supervisor know what his group is doing to catch up and, second, to let the supervisor know that his team deserves recognition for its initiative. If you're a team leader, one of your most important functions is to communicate the group's progress or decisions or actions to the world outside the group.

18. *Maintaining.* Another important team leader function is to provide materials and perform the routine tasks that keep the team functioning without a hitch, such as ordering raw materials in time to keep production up to standard.

Some groups can become overly task-oriented to the point of becoming dysfunctional. Members of an overly task-oriented team often feel ground down and burned out because nothing is more important than "making the numbers."

Process Dynamics

To prevent a team from becoming overly task-oriented and to keep the team healthy, everyone on the team has to manage its process dynamics. Some people call these aspects of teamwork "maintenance functions" because they help a team maintain the relationships within the group necessary to achieve its task-oriented goals. A group maintains itself and keeps itself healthy by paying attention to how the team achieves its objectives and how the members relate to each other, as well as to the feelings that people in the group have for one another and for the group. Consider the following ten functions:

1. *Gatekeeping.* Andy, Mac, and Sue all showed concern for how the group functioned by taking an interest in other people's opinions or feelings. They opened the channels of communication; they ensured that everyone who wanted to, even Al, could express an opinion—whether anyone liked that opinion or not.

2. *Listening.* If you open the gate, then it's your responsibility to pay attention to what comes through it—whether or not you like what you hear. Everyone listened to Al, even if he or she didn't agree with him.

3. *Expediting.* Sometimes gatekeeping and listening can get your team off track. Expediting crosses the line between task and process by keeping discussions on track, while encouraging everyone to contribute. That's why Andy asked whether there were any other ideas.

4. *Encouraging.* You discourage people by cutting them off or by putting down or discounting what they have to say. No one did that to Al. The team members disagreed with him, but they encouraged him to speak up by looking for an alternative to overtime that would satisfy him *and* the needs of the group.

5. *Empowering.* Andy has the power he needs to make decisions—the status power that comes with the job. He shares his power by encouraging others to make decisions and to do things for themselves.

6. *Harmonizing.* Sue created harmony by

coming up with the answer to the question of how to get back on the productivity track. You harmonize by negotiating, reconciling, or mediating disagreements. You can also relieve tension with appropriate humor.

7. *Yielding.* Al created roadblocks, but, in the end, he realized that his was an unpopular viewpoint, which he was willing to give up for the team's sake. Andy, by not dominating the team, yielded status. Fred yielded by admitting that he might not be up to speed. You yield any time you're willing to meet people halfway.

8. *Observing.* Looking and listening are only two parts of effective observing. You also have to pay attention to the group's process and alert the group to any possible damage to effective functioning that you see. One way to do this is to express feelings you see in the group. This technique is called *mirroring.* Mac performed the observing function when he checked to see if the group agreed with Al about overtime. Other ways to observe are to call attention to group reactions to what is going on and by diagnosing problems reflected in group behavior.

9. *Accepting.* The group clearly accepted Al and Fred, even though Al created some roadblocks to group decision making and Fred felt unequal to the task. When you respect people's rights to express themselves and to meet their own needs, they reciprocate by respecting yours. You also need to respect and even promote differences among people in the group in order to begin a rational problem-solving process.

10. *Cheerleading.* Everyone has to help the team feel good about itself, about how it functions, and about the successes it achieves. Both

Mac's reference to pride and Sue's comment about productivity bonuses are cheerleading activities. And what do you think Andy accomplished by saying, "You guys did a great job"?

An overly process-oriented team, like an overly task-oriented team, can self-destruct. Getting bogged down in maintaining relationships leads to the creation of a social club: It's fun to work there, but you won't be working for long.

Appropriate attention to both task and process dynamics at all stages of a team's development moves the team toward success in working together and in reaching goals. A healthy team is both productive and pleasant to belong to. And a healthy team is one in which everyone takes an active role in managing what is done and how it is done.

CHAPTER SIX

How to Encourage Open, Honest, and Direct Communication

Andy's team is too good to be true, right? People just don't work together that well, not in the real world. Or do they?

What has Andy done that's so remarkable? Think back over the dialogues you've read, and try to find just one thing that you think is impossible to do. Work groups do exist in which you can find the kind of open, honest, and direct communication that characterizes Andy's team—that characterizes all effective teams. But that kind of communication, those channels and linkages, don't just happen; they have to be created.

A month after Fred came on the job, Andy had him close down his work area thirty minutes early and report to his office, just to talk about how things are going.

Andy: So, how are things going, Fred?

Fred [*unenthusiastically*]: Pretty good, I guess.

Andy [*aware of Fred's lack of enthusiasm*]: That doesn't sound all that confident.

Fred: No. They're okay.

Andy: Your productivity's right on the money. I've no complaints, but from the way you're talking, something seems to be bothering you.

Fred: I appreciate the help you and Mac have given me. The group really works well as a team. I've never worked in a place like this. And, you know, I've never worked for anyone so quick to pay a compliment, so all that's okay.

Andy [*filling a few seconds of hesitation*]: But?

Fred: You'll think I'm crazy.

Andy: All of us here are a little nuts or we wouldn't do this kind of work.

Fred [*laughing*]: Well, I may be nuttier than most. [*after a pause*] Andy, I'm bored. Only a month on the job, and I feel like I'm doing the same thing every minute of the day.

Andy: You are.

Fred [*surprised*]: What?

Andy: You're doing the same thing every minute of the day. We all are. It's these contracts. They have us pushing out frame joints by the thousands. What would you rather be doing?

Fred: I'd like to get out on the construction site, work on the frame itself.

Andy: Let's talk about it. Tell me more.

Fred: I've done some outside work before, you know—oil rigs, high-rises. I feel a whole lot more energetic working out there.

Andy: You're feeling confined.

Fred: Yeah. And I thought I'd be able to adjust, but I'm not doing such a hot job of it.

Andy: What do you want to do about how you're feeling?

Fred: I don't know. I understand you worked the frames before you got promoted. Got any suggestions?

Andy: No, not really. My circumstances were different. Besides, it's your feelings, and we have to concentrate only on them.

Most people are reluctant to communicate with their leaders and with one another. What can you do to get Andy's kind of communication going?

Encouraging Dialogue

What Andy does that you can also do is to encourage dialogue by opening doors—what we call gatekeeping. Notice that we don't use the word *discussion*, which implies chitchat. We mean *dialogue*: the exchange and the examination of important opinions or information between two people. And once Andy opens the gate, he follows the suggestions listed in the box, all of which are steps that you can take to encourage and sustain dialogue in the group.

When it comes to communication, everyone can be a team leader. But each person has to take responsibility for ensuring that open, honest, and direct communication takes place all the time and in all directions—up, down, and sideways.

- *Listen actively.* You listen actively when you clear your mind and your desk of all distractions and participate in what the other person is saying without diverting attention to yourself. You show your interest by asking questions or probing for information. Nodding your head and asking the other person to continue are both things you can

Steps for Encouraging Dialogue

1. Actively listen without diverting attention to yourself.
2. Accept advice and give it only when solicited or when appropriate.
3. Be candid, and accept candor.
4. Become conscious of nonverbal behavior—your own, as well as that of other people.
5. Manage your own way of speaking; be clear, be complete, but also be concise and to the point.
6. Provide information, and accept information from others (and give them credit for it).
7. Be patient with and encourage disagreement.
8. Express feelings appropriately, and acknowledge other people's.

---

do to encourage another person to speak. Andy did all of those things in the previous dialogue.

▪ *Accept and give advice.* Before people will graciously accept advice from you, they have to feel (1) that you have a sincere interest in their concerns and (2) that you're willing to accept advice from other people. Active listening helps you communicate your interest; only if you actually accept advice from other people will they be convinced of your openness. Another way to have your advice accepted is to offer it only when it's solicited or when it's appropriate to offer it. Andy showed his genuine interest and refused to give advice when it was solicited because he felt it was inappropriate to do so.

- *Be candid and accept candor.* Many people love to tell you "the truth," but often they themselves can't accept the truth—especially if the truth's about them. Andy has coached people to believe that he's candid by being candid, but he has also coached them to be candid by being open to their candor and by actively listening to them when they are. How far do you think you'll get if every time someone tries to open up to you, especially about their feelings about themselves or about you, you say, "I don't want to hear it"?

- *Become conscious of nonverbal behavior.* As important as words are to human communication, they constitute less than 10 percent of human communication. Andy "heard" Fred's feelings in his tone of voice. You "see" people's feelings in their faces. You can often tell if what people say is true just by the way their eyes hold yours; experts tell us that wandering eyes reflect either a lack of confidence in what we're saying or a consciousness that what we're saying isn't true. To become an effective communicator, study your own nonverbal behavior by listening to yourself speak on an audiotape or by watching yourself in a videotape or in a mirror. These are very revealing techniques. Watch other people as well. Become conscious of how they express themselves in nonverbal ways.

- *Manage your own way of speaking.* Andy makes himself clear as often as he can (no one's perfect). He's as complete as he has to be, but he's concise and to the point. To practice speaking that way, you can write out things you want to say and then read your words aloud to hear how they sound. You can also build your vocabulary and look for clear, short expressions to use in making your point. Finally, measure your "air time," that is, see how long it takes you to speak your piece. Use a tape recorder, or have a valued, trusted person time you and give you feedback.

- *Provide and accept information.* It's important to effective communication that you share with others any relevant data that will help you, them as individuals, and the team as a whole to succeed. Individuals and the team both need your information and will resent your withholding it. They will also resent your unwillingness to listen to and accept information they have for you or the team. And they will definitely resent your failure to give them credit for the information they provide you.

- *Be patient with and encouraging disagreement.* Recall the dialogue in Chapter 5, when Al disagreed with other team members about the importance of being on schedule. No one liked what Al said, but nobody cut him off. Al and the team disagreed and agreed to disagree—and Al finally accepted the team's viewpoint. You can't expect people to be patient with your opinions unless you're patient with theirs. You don't have to agree, but you might, to paraphrase a famous quotation, defend to the death people's right to their opinions and feelings.

- *Express and acknowledge feelings.* Hiding feelings—what we call "sandbagging"—can totally destroy a team. Andy doesn't let anyone, including himself, hide feelings that could disrupt the team's effectiveness and its productivity. He probes for and mirrors feelings (e.g., "You're feeling confined"). You can do the same, but remember two key words: "appropriately" and "acknowledge." Ranting and raving when you're upset and shouting and doing handsprings when you're elated may not be the best ways of expressing yourself under most conditions in the workplace. Ignoring what other people are feeling may also be a sure way of killing your relationships.

Anyone can follow these steps to increase the effectiveness of his or her own, as well as the group's, communication, but there's one thing that a team leader does that other people on the team may not have to do—communicate effectively with people or groups outside the team. That's a team leader function.

When you, as the team leader, tell people outside the group—for example, top management—what the group is doing, how the group is doing it, and what the group needs or requires to be effective, your actions give team members confidence in you and in themselves. They know they're being well represented to people who need to know what they're about.

Representing other people to the group is equally important. Knowing what is happening outside the group helps team members relate themselves to organizational goals and objectives, clarifies expectations of what they're to do and how, and explains the needs or requirements of the organization as a whole.

Giving the group information that you get from outside the team makes it possible for the team members to use that information to make themselves more successful. Sometimes the team has no conduit to outside information other than what you, as its leader, can supply.

People do work together in the real world the way Andy's team does. There's nothing remarkable about it. To work together that well requires open, honest, and direct communication, but achieving that kind of communication requires effort. Adopting the guidelines we've covered here will help you create the open communication you seek.

CHAPTER SEVEN

How to Resolve Conflict and Other Team Problems

We've already seen that not everything in Andy's work team comes up roses. Al doesn't want to work overtime and doesn't have the same respect for the bottom line that his teammates have. After only a month, Fred is bored with his job and wants to move outside. You'd think that with all his management skills, Andy wouldn't have to deal with such issues. But that's the whole point. Because of his skills, he does deal with such issues and, in so doing, keeps his team healthy. He manages the team's problems, rather than suppressing or ignoring them.

And it's not just Andy. Remember the way Sue and Mac dealt with Al's issues back in Chapter 5? They confronted his unwillingness to take on overtime and came up with an alternative solution that benefited everyone. They also confronted his lack of concern for the team's productivity goals. They assumed leadership roles. So where was Andy?

Andy supported the team's willingness to deal with its own issues and encouraged the members to work out their differences. A team leader is not required to satisfy every need the team may have. However, unless the team has members like Sue and Mac, the leader has to step in and fill the leadership vacuum.

Again, open, honest, and direct communication prevents disagreements from erupting into conflicts. It makes it easier to recognize symptoms of conflict. It prevents groupthink that seeks to maintain group harmony at all costs. It enables teams to confront their problems and to take steps to solve them.

Symptoms of Conflict

You need to be conscious of the possibility of conflict in teams. The symptoms aren't all that difficult to recognize. Here are three common ones.

1. *Bickering.* Do your teammates bicker a lot, often over trivial matters? Sometimes, the inability to get along signals an organizational problem; perhaps people are in jobs for which they're not suited or in which they're not interested, or perhaps organizational changes have not been planned or implemented properly. Sometimes the inability to get along signals interpersonal problems that have not surfaced directly. Somewhere along the line, someone has to stop bickering long enough to ask, "Why are we bickering all the time? What's at the bottom of it?"

2. *Apathy.* Bickering can also indicate apathy, but the bickering looks a little different. Apathy is often manifested by nitpicking and bickering for no apparent reason, and it's accompanied by other destructive behaviors you can recognize.

A sense of tedium permeates your work. You or other people feel bored, but not the way Fred, who wanted more exciting, more challenging work, did. Ennui settles over an apathetic group, a feeling of weariness and discontent. Look around your team. Do the people complain of being tired and unhappy over their work, even though they're not really working hard enough to wear themselves out?

An apathetic group experiences a slowdown in the work. Individuals and the group as a whole miss deadlines. The group experiences increases in physical ailments and absenteeism. Has that been happening to your group? Take note of how much complaining, absenteeism, and tardiness exist. They may signal serious problems.

And if you're the supervisor, you know you and the group are in serious trouble when *you* lose the desire to come to work in the morning.

3. *Groupthink.* Sometimes apathy produces groupthink because no one wants to "swim upstream." But usually groupthink occurs when fear causes decisions to be based mainly on an overriding desire to maintain group harmony at all costs. Decisions are made by concurrence and compliance, rather than by consensus. Groupthink was operating in President John F. Kennedy's cabinet when it decided to go ahead with the Bay of Pigs invasion in 1961, despite intelligence warning them that the operation was doomed to fail.

As in the Kennedy cabinet example, groupthink often results from a strength that is carried to a dysfunctional extreme. The Kennedy cabinet worked together so well and had so much respect for the president and his brilliance that it failed to challenge its own assumptions. It exhibited a "three monkeys mentality": See no evil, hear no evil, speak no evil. If no one is speaking up in your group, even though people see things that are going wrong, you may be victims of groupthink.

However, the most common groupthink situation in business is the "If it ain't broke, don't fix it" mentality. Why monkey around (pun intended) with what's working? If you or your teammates don't look at what could be improved, your group will stagnate and will lose out to competitors who do tinker with what works. Just ask any representative of the automobile industry in the United States.

If you work for a well-established organization with a long and glorious history, you're likely to run into the "That's not how we do it" mentality. Businessman Ross Perot has said that that's what happened when General Motors bought his company, Electronic Data Systems, from him and placed him on the GM board of directors. In his version of the story, when he complained about how things were done at GM, he was told, "If it ain't broke, don't fix it." He was also told to quiet down; that going public with problems was "not how we do it." (While history shows that he was right about the problems he saw, many people still disagree with him about whether he had any real solutions to them.)

Solving Problems

Solving problems is a primary purpose of open, direct, and honest communication in a team. The only way to solve team problems is to confront them—not by bickering, not by apathetically ignoring them, and not by avoiding them through groupthink. But what kinds of problems can your team fix?

A team can rarely solve a problem we call *self-centered.* This type of problem falls entirely on the individual affected or on the group supervisor or leader. Self-centered problems usually affect only one person. Often time is too short to call in the group; sometimes only one person has the skills, the knowledge, or the opportunity to "fix the problem." Fred's boredom, along with his desire to move outside, is a self-centered problem; Andy can listen to him, but it's unlikely that he can do anything to help him. When it's your problem, it's your problem.

Other problems are *organizational* problems that originate within the group or that affect some process inside it. Such problems are best taken up by the group or by the subgroup affected by them. Al's problems fall into this category, because in this case one person on the team can have a very negative effect on the team's success. (Yes, Fred's problem could have negative consequences—if he doesn't make some personal decisions and adjustments.) The team has a stake in helping Al make some important decisions about the unit's goals and about his work and his relationships with other people. Andy will have to take a hand in helping the team coach Al.

Although it is easy to recognize that something is wrong, it's not always as easy to identify what that something is or what to do about it. Some problems are well defined, clear, and unambiguous and are connected by cause-and-effect relationships; such problems can be solved by analytic methods. Other problems are poorly defined, or diffuse, and are cloaked in values, attitudes, perceptions, assumptions, or meanings. These problems are often just sensed and do not lend themselves well to analytic techniques; instead, they must be approached from a different (lateral) direction.*

Regardless of the type of problem or the approach the team has to take, problem-solving activities begin with open, honest, and direct communication. It's the only way for you to get a comprehensive picture of what is going on. In a majority of cases, five steps will help you do what is necessary.

1. *Collect data.* Compare what things should be like with how things are (e.g., a standard production rate is 150 joints a day, but Fred's actual performance is 125 joints a day).

2. *Develop a preliminary statement of the problem.* Express the problem as an unfavorable relationship between what is planned and what is actually happening (e.g., Fred's performance is at only 83.3 percent of acceptable standards).

3. *Ask open-ended questions.* Questions that begin with *when, who, where, what, why,* and *how* help identify contributing factors (e.g., when did his production slip? What happened just before his production slipped?).

*For more information on how to manage problem identification and problem solving, see Donald H. Weiss, *Creative Problem Solving,* Successful Office Skills series (New York: AMACOM, 1988).

4. *Look for contributing factors.* Contributing factors may actually be the "cause" of the problem (e.g., just before his productivity fell, Fred complained of being bored with his job).

5. *Restate the problem.* The final statement of the problem can often suggest its solution (e.g., Fred's bad feelings about his job have led to a slowdown in productivity).

Fred's self-centered problem has affected the team. It has now become an organizational problem. If you were Andy, what do you think you would do?

Taking action on problems that affect the team is essential to the team's effectiveness. If you let a serious problem fester, you may undermine everything that you and your teammates are attempting to achieve. Your open, honest, and direct communication, on the other hand, helps keep disagreements from erupting into conflicts. You can help identify the causes of the team's problems, and you can help the team confront any barriers to its success and take steps to overcome them.

Conclusion

Not every work unit is a team; perhaps yours shouldn't be one. But most groups and their members benefit from teamwork.

To create real teamwork, you and your teammates have to make a conscious effort to become effective—at creating synergy. This requires doing what has to be done to get the results you're after—managing your task dynamics. It also requires monitoring how you do what has to be done—managing your process dynamics. This is done through open, honest, and direct communication. That same kind of communication is needed to bring conflicts to the surface and to resolve them, as well as to identify the real causes of problems and to solve them.

It takes talent to make a team successful, but that's not enough. All that talent has to come together synergistically in order for the team to reach its primary goal. Just ask the Chicago Cubs.

Suggested Readings

Buchholz, Steve, and Thomas Roth. *Creating the High-Performance Team.* Edited by Karen Hess. New York: John Wiley & Sons, 1987.

Burck, Charles G. "What Happens When Workers Manage Themselves." *Fortune,* July 27, 1981, pp. 62–69.

Dumaine, Brian. "Who Needs a Boss?" *Fortune,* May 7, 1990, pp. 52–60.

Harper, Bob, and Ann Harper. *Succeeding as a Self-Directed Work Team.* King of Prussia, Penn.: Organization Design and Development, 1989.

Lee, Chris. "Beyond Teamwork." *Training,* June 1990, pp. 26ff.

Osborn, Jack, et al. *Self-Directed Work Teams: The*

New American Challenge. Homewood, Ill.: businessOne Irwin, 1990.

Ouchi, William. *The M-Form Society: How American Teamwork Can Recapture the Competitive Edge*. Reading, Mass.: Addison-Wesley, 1984.

Senge, Peter M. *The Fifth Discipline: The Art and Practice of The Learning Organization*. New York: Doubleday Currency, 1986.

Weiss, Donald H. *How To Build High Performance Teams*. Watertown, Mass.: American Management Association, 1991.

Index

About the Author

Donald H. Weiss, Ph.D., is CEO of Self-Management Communications, Inc., St. Louis, and a well-known author of books, videos, and cassette-workbook programs that focus on management and interpersonal skills. He has been a senior training and development executive and consultant for more than twenty-five years. Among his corporate positions were: program manager for the Citicorp Executive Development Center and corporate training manager for Millers' Mutual Insurance. His many publications include fifteen previous books in the SOS series and *Fair, Square, and Legal: Safe Hiring, Managing, and Firing Practices to Keep Your Company Out of Court* (all AMACOM). Dr. Weiss earned his Ph.D. from Tulane University.